THE FINAL QUESTION OF JESUS

LIFECHANGE BOOKS

JOE STOWELL

Multnomah®Publishers *Sisters, Oregon*

THE FINAL QUESTION OF JESUS
published by Multnomah Publishers, Inc.

© 2004 by Dr. Joseph M. Stowell

International Standard Book Number: 1-59052-204-4

Cover design by Design Concepts/Kevin Keller
Cover image by Getty Images/Gary S. and Vivian Chapman

Unless otherwise indicated, Scripture quotations are from:
New American Standard Bible
© 1960, 1977, 1995 by the Lockman Foundation

Other Scripture quotations:
The Holy Bible, New King James Version (NKJV)
© 1984 by Thomas Nelson, Inc.
The Message © 1993 by Eugene H. Peterson

Multnomah is a trademark of Multnomah Publishers, Inc.,
and is registered in the U.S. Patent and Trademark Office.
The colophon is a trademark of Multnomah Publishers, Inc.

Printed in the United States of America

For information:
MULTNOMAH PUBLISHERS, INC.
POST OFFICE BOX 1720
SISTERS, OREGON 97759

Library of Congress Cataloging-in-Publication Data
Stowell, Joseph M.
The final question of Jesus / Joseph M. Stowell.
p. cm.
ISBN 1-59052-204-4
1. Christian life--Baptist authors. I. Title.
BV4501.3.S769 2004
248.4--dc22   2004009831

04 05 06 07 08 09—10 9 8 7 6 5 4 3 2 1 0

To my friends,

Tim and Eileen Ostrander
whose passion for people has
brought a healing and helping touch
in the name of Jesus.

Table of Contents

THE STORY

After these things Jesus manifested Himself again to the disciples at the Sea of Tiberias, and He manifested Himself in this way. Simon Peter, and Thomas called Didymus, and Nathanael of Cana in Galilee, and the sons of Zebedee, and two others of His disciples were together. Simon Peter said to them, "I am going fishing." They said to him, "We will also come with you." They went out and got into the boat; and that night they caught nothing.

But when the day was now breaking, Jesus stood on the beach; yet the disciples did not know that it was Jesus. So Jesus said to them, "Children, you do not have any fish, do you?" They answered Him, "No." And He said to them, "Cast the net on the right-hand side of the boat and you will find a catch." So they cast, and then they were not able to haul it in because of the great number of *fish. Therefore that disciple whom Jesus loved said to Peter, "It is the Lord." So when Simon Peter heard that it was the Lord, he put his outer garment on (for he was stripped for work), and threw himself into the sea. But the other disciples came in the little boat, for they were not far from the land, but about one hundred yards away, dragging the net full of fish.*

So when they got out on the land, they saw a charcoal fire already laid and fish placed on it, and bread. Jesus said to them, "Bring some of the fish which you have now caught." Simon Peter went up and drew the net to land, full of large fish, a hundred and fifty-three; and although there were so many, the net was not torn. Jesus said to them, "Come and have breakfast." None of the disciples ventured to question Him, "Who are You?" knowing that it was the Lord. Jesus came and took the bread and gave it to them, and the fish likewise. This is now the third time that Jesus was manifested to the disciples, after He was raised from the dead.

So when they had finished breakfast, Jesus said to Simon Peter, "Simon, son of John, do you love Me more than these?" He said to Him, "Yes, Lord; You know that I love You." He said to him, "Tend My lambs." He said to him again a second time, "Simon, son of John, do you love Me?" He said to Him, "Yes, Lord; You know that I love You." He said to him, "Shepherd My sheep." He said to him the third time, "Simon, son of John, do you love Me?" Peter was grieved because He said to him the third time, "Do you love Me?" And he said to Him, "Lord, You know all things; You know that I love You." Jesus said to him, "Tend My sheep." (John 21:1–17)

Chapter One

THE ULTIMATE QUESTION

…and your answer is?

There are two words that you should never say to Jesus.

They are *I quit!*

But if you do, He will not ask you why. His question will be far more personal. Far more penetrating.

We all know how awkward it is to be asked questions that put us on the spot…

…Do you know why I pulled you over?

…Have you heard anything that I have said?

…Could you give me your PIN number, please?

…Do you know where your ball just landed?

…And just how do you intend to support my daughter?

But count on it, there will never be a more unsettling question than the question Jesus wants to ask you. It's the final question that Jesus asked Peter.

"Simon, son of John, do you love Me?"

And Christ didn't ask just once. He asked twice. And then yet a third time. It was like driving a nail deep into Peter's already wounded soul.

If my wife, Martie, looked deeply into my eyes—with longing in her own and said, "Do you love me?"

My answer would be quick and predictable. "Of course!"

But what if she refused to be satisfied with such a routine reply? Suppose she asked yet again, with emotion breaking her voice, "No, I really need to know, do you *love me?*" And before I could get a grip on what was going on, imagine her asking me a third time, with even more urgency, "Joe…please…do you love me?"

I would know something deep was going on. It would be clear to me that under her words, something big was brewing. Something that needed my full attention.

That had to be how Peter felt as Jesus questioned him in the early morning mist on the seashore, after an exhausting—and completely fruitless—night of fishing.

Which is what makes Christ's interrogation of Peter particularly disturbing. You're probably aware that Jesus never asks questions because he doesn't know the answer. He asks questions to make a point—to draw out the hidden, inner issues of life, and to press us to readjust. Jesus was probing Peter's heart in the face of his recent decision to turn his back on the "people business" and return to his former career of fishing. This was the career from which Jesus had called him three short years earlier, recruiting him to a new enterprise: giving his life for people. Or, as Jesus put it, fishing for men!

Peter had bailed on Jesus, and Jesus took it personally—as He always does when we say, "I quit!" Could it be that Peter no longer loved his Lord? Or was he just totally fogged out by a dismal sense of discouragement and failure?

Christ's call to focus Peter's life on the needs and nurture of people is not an isolated moment in history. If you call yourself a follower of Jesus, it is His call in your life as well. His invitation to "follow Me" is always connected to a daily commitment to touch lives for His sake—stepping boldly and lovingly into the world of those we encounter on a daily basis. You can't have one without the other.

When Jesus came to our planet, His life was always about people. If, then, you are determined to follow Him, don't be surprised that the adventure will lead you neck-deep into the needs of people. And when you go off calling as Peter did, He will want to know what happened to your love for Him.

He will ask, "Do you love Me?"

If your answer is yes, Lord, you know that I love You—as Peter answered—expect to hear Him say, "Then tend My lambs!"

And by the way, His concern about our love for Him and for the people He places in our lives is not an ethereal "church thought" that has a nice ring to it. His question presses us to focus our lives and resources on the passion that is closest to His heart, the most valuable commodity on this planet...*people!*

Which people? People who need the healing touch that only our acts of love can give. People who will thrive on the gift of our time and attention. People whose eternal destinies lie in the balance—this very moment. People who need to have their past mistakes canceled and their future given back to them because we have forgiven them. People who need a good word of comfort, whose lives are waiting for someone who will really care. People who need space, not suffocation; who need to be loved, not used; blessed, not manipulated; prayed for and helped, not slandered. People who need to be rescued from the snares of the evil one. People who are distressed and harassed like sheep without a shepherd.

Believe me, if you hang out with people there is no shortage of opportunities to prove to Jesus how much you love Him. People are everywhere. We are a needy bunch.

If only it were a little easier....

Jan had worked across from an empty desk for weeks. Sally, who had occupied that desk for years, had recently been promoted to the executive floor.

Quite frankly, Jan was relieved.

When she had come to the job, she was looking forward to making a few new friends. In close range at the neighboring desk, Sally was an obvious prospect. She was pretty, fun, and aggressively into office politics. It didn't take long, however, to see that this was a woman determined to move her career forward—at any cost. In short, people were only important to her if they could help her on her trajectory toward senior management.

Jan had no idea of the buzz saw she was walking into as she ventured into what she assumed was a "Christ-like relationship" with Sally.

When Sally spent too much time in the cafeteria, schmoozing with the up-and-comers, Jan willingly picked up her work. She covered for Sally when the boss called and she wasn't at her desk. Jan did whatever she could to prove to Sally that she was a trusted friend. They often went out for dinner after work. Jan listened and gave whatever input she could, as Sally would take most of the evening talking about herself and her struggles with guys.

Jan was a new follower of Jesus. Soon after becoming a

Christian, she had learned that to authenticate her love and relationship with her Lord, she needed to intentionally climb out of her own world and become involved in the lives of others. Sally, in her mind, was a prime opportunity to do just that. In fact, Jan often prayed that her interest in and support for Sally might lead Sally to become interested in a relationship with Jesus.

Jan was good at what she did in the office. In fact it wasn't long before the "powers that be" began to target her for corporate advancement. The thought of this was too much for Sally, and she began to look at Jan differently— as a threat to her career dreams. After two years of building their friendship, Jan overheard a conversation between Sally and the boss that shocked her to the core. In a sad, reluctant voice, Sally explained how much of Jan's work she'd had to pick up and correct before it could be submitted. Jan, Sally said, spent too much time with friends on the phone, and when corrected for it would always have a few choice comments about the weird way that upper management ran the business.

None of it was true.

But Sally had been clever enough to work the system, and it was Sally who got the promotion. Jan was stuck at the same desk with a tarnished reputation.

In Jan's mind, this thing about loving Jesus by reaching out to people hadn't worked out the way she thought it would. As it turned out, people weren't simply needy, they were *dangerous.* She had been used, hurt, and discarded. Deeply discouraged—not only with people, but with Jesus who had asked her to get sacrificially involved with others— Jan was now determined to take life into her own hands. She would manage whomever landed at Sally's desk in a way that would guarantee her own safety and personal advance in the corporation.

Jan's heart was no longer ready to reach out for Jesus' sake. She had learned her lesson the hard way. It was now time for her to get on the corporate train and make something of her life. She would play everything close to her vest, and keep everything on a professional level aimed at her own best interest. Life was too short, she told herself, and she didn't need the grief of another people disaster in her life.

It wasn't that she was ready to totally deny Jesus. She still gladly attended her weekly small group meetings, worshiped with enthusiasm on Sunday, and took copious notes as the pastor shared his heart. It's just that Jan had become a little more savvy in the marketplace. Jesus would just have to understand that. His way didn't really work at the office. She even wondered if perhaps the world of two thousand years ago was nicer than "office world," and that if Jesus were here today He too might revise some of His thoughts about the place and importance of people.

So, when Heather replaced Sally at the nearby desk, Jan was ready.

Heather was pleasant, easy to be around, and openly friendly to Jan. It crossed Jan's mind that Sally was like that in the beginning as well. What Jan *didn't* know was that Heather was close to a transition point in life. She had recently been deeply impressed by the unconditional love and concern of a couple of Christian friends. When Heather heard through the office grapevine that Jan was a Christian, she was secretly pleased. She was anxious to experience another relationship that would bless her with the selfless love she had experienced from her other friends. In fact, Heather had often thought (though she didn't let on to her friends) that Jesus was becoming increasingly attractive to her. She was drawn by their talk of His sacrificial and forgiving love. She had experienced it from them, and knew deep down how much she needed to be forgiven.

Warmly and expectantly, Heather made attempts to get to know Jan. She would ask, "Could we go on break together? Or how about lunch?" But Jan made sure that she was always busy. Conversations were polite, but Jan's brief answers guaranteed that they didn't get much traction.

Jan felt good about the distance.

Jan had no clue.

Countless followers of Jesus, like Jan, have "had it" with people.

—Wives jilted by faithless husbands.

—Men embittered by game-playing women.

—Children deeply disappointed by parents.

—Parents stinging from rejection by their own children.

—Customers cheated by fellow Christians in the business world.

—Teenage girls sexually molested by an abusive dad— who also happened to be an elder in the church.

—People tired of dead-end, nonreciprocal, one-way relationships.

—Wounded people who have been betrayed by a friend.

—People who find life easier to manage when lived on their own terms.

—People who have found that most people are nice, but not necessary.

The list goes on. At one time or another, all of us have found our fellow human beings to be disappointing and discouraging. Most of us feel like "amening" the philosopher who wrote, "The more I get to know people, the more I like my dog!"

So…forgetting that our purpose in life is to prove our love to Jesus by staying involved in the lives of others for their good (even if it costs us something), we tend to do what Peter did…bail on Jesus and recoil into the tidy comfort of life on our own terms.

Chapter Two

READY TO QUIT

...living with the urge to give up on people

I have a confession to make. I am *not* the kind of person who tends to find people to be a problem. I am an unrepentant, hopelessly addicted people-person!

I know. That confession is a turnoff to those of you who view my personality type with a measure of disdain. I understand, but for reasons best known to Himself, God has sprinkled folks like me throughout the world—people who feed on interaction with other humans. We're like Golden Labs when someone approaches, be it friend or stranger.

But if the truth were known, we people-persons find others satisfying to us as long as those "others" feed our appetites. We tend not to listen well, unless the conversation is about us. We overpromise and underperform. Any sacrificial extensions of our time and resources that don't reward us will rarely be attempted again. In fact (though we would be the last to admit it), we can actually *neglect* the legitimate needs of others—including our own family—when our people need is being satisfied with someone else. And when the current company we're in causes us more hassle than they're worth, we have been known to move on to more interesting people.

What really lies under the outer layers of a people-person (if we aren't careful), is the full-blown capacity to use others for our own emotional satisfaction, instead of truly loving others to prove our love for Christ.

In the end, people-persons are just as liable to avoid significant and sacrificial interaction with members of the human family as your favorite recluse.

None of us are exempt. We are costrugglers in a battle to stay "on calling" as followers of Jesus.

I've always been fascinated by the triple interrogation that Jesus put Peter through in John 21. Actually, *convicted* might be a more accurate description of how I feel.

Imagine a face-to-face encounter with Jesus, the almighty Creator, who keeps asking you a single question with that penetrating gaze that cuts to the very depths of your soul.

The question?

"Do you love Me?"

What was Jesus after?

Jesus was after Peter's love.

What was Peter's problem?

Peter had had it with life on Jesus' terms!

And isn't that exactly our dilemma when people prove to be less rewarding than we thought they would be? Peter had just flat-out become *discouraged* as a follower of Jesus.

Actually, Peter had had it with just about everyone. Including the Lord! Before His death and resurrection, Jesus had been with Peter and the disciples 24/7/365/3. All of Peter's hopes had been pegged on the Teacher from Galilee. He had given up a prosperous career in fishing to follow Jesus into the world of people. He could remember with such clarity the day when Jesus called to him: "Follow Me, and I will make you a fisher of men!"

For three years Peter basked in the passionate love that Jesus poured out to people of all kinds. From prostitutes to princes, outcasts to the highly connected, lepers to doctors, children and women. His whole world was about people, their needs, and their transition into His kingdom.

Then the dream exploded.

Jesus had gotten them all in trouble by agitating the authorities to the point of a mob action against Him.

After the resurrection, Peter thought that it would be back to the way it used to be. But that never materialized. Before Jesus questioned Peter on that morning by the sea, He had only shown up twice. Things just weren't turning out like Peter thought they should. (Ever feel that way in your walk with Jesus?)

And this thing about being in the enterprise of people…that seemed to be in the tank as well. Who would want anything to do with followers of Jesus now that He had died as a disgraced criminal rather than conquering as a victorious King?

For most people, the resurrection was no more than a rumor. The "headliner" was out of public circulation, and the crowds had long ago dispersed. To make matters worse, the authorities were still "ticked" about the near insurrection Jesus had caused. And the disciples were being accused of stealing His body.

The risks of being in the people business were just too high, and the list of reasons to bail was long.

On top of all that, Peter wasn't feeling too good about himself the morning that Jesus showed up on the beach. How could he forget his total collapse in Caiaphas's courtyard when pressed about his association with Jesus?

The more he thought about it, the more he realized he just wasn't cut out for the calling of Christ in his life. People and their needs would just have to take second place! Peter was going fishing—and taking Thomas, James, John, Nathaniel, and two other disciples with him as partners in his fledgling business. It was back to life as usual. Back to something he could control. Back to the well-practiced tasks of catching, counting, and selling fish. Back to the comfortable routine of repairing boats and mending nets.

In simple terms, Peter said, "I quit!"

You know the feeling. How often have you just wanted to quit? Quit parenting. Quit the hassle of a difficult marriage. Quit trying to communicate with that cantankerous coworker. Quit being so nice to people who aren't all that nice to you. Quit leading your small group. Quit the challenges of following Jesus into the lives of needy, fickle, ungrateful, demanding, critical, consuming people. Quit forgiving. Quit giving people "the benefit of the doubt."

More subtly, as we continue to go though the motions, a lot of us have already quit inside. We dutifully live out our marriage obligations, parent, help others, and perform our routines with a sense of grumpy obligation. We spend our mental energy dreaming of a better life. We are tempted to flirt around the edges of an affair, lose ourselves in a novel, or escape into the fantasy universe of the Web. What we really want is life on our own terms. A life where we can be in control, and manage the outcomes to our own satisfaction. A life where others care about us instead of our having to care about them.

If you are now or have ever been gripped by thoughts like these, take heart! You are not alone.

It's exactly where Peter was on the night when he and his buddies climbed back into the old fishing boat. Compared to the recent disappointments of following Christ, the thought of fishing had a compelling draw. You can almost hear Peter thinking, *At least this is something I can succeed at.*

Think again. Peter was soon to find out that life on our own terms is ultimately a hollow and futile endeavor.

That very first night of fishing they caught nothing. It's no big deal if you get "skunked" on vacation, but if it's the first day of your new business, it's a major blow. If Peter had been discouraged before, he must have been devastated by the time the morning sun sent its first tentative rays across the sea.

Mark it down. It is no coincidence that in the midst of Peter's discouragement and emptiness of life, Jesus showed up on the beach. The Lord who had called him, called him once again, urging him back to the mission that he had given up on. Back to the sometimes messy and always challenging business of shepherding people. But more importantly, back into a love relationship with Him.

As I type these words into my laptop, buckled into my seat 35,000 feet over the Atlantic, I find my heart praying for you. Praying that as you read these words you will slow down and sense that Jesus is right now showing up on the beach of your heart. Calling you to follow Him once again. Calling to you in the midst of your reasons to quit, discouragements, and failures. Calling you back to Himself. Back to the passion that drives His heart to this day...the needs and nurture of people.

You've got to be struck by the fact that Jesus didn't show up that morning as the divine taskmaster, sternly informing Peter that he was AWOL, and that he needed to get back to kingdom work. In Jesus' mind, the central issue was not about the task. It was about Peter's love for Him.

Every time we find ourselves ready to bail, we must remind ourselves that the people business is not about the duty of it all, but about our love for Him. This is why Jesus takes it personally when we climb back into our own self-centered world.

By the way, if you think this story is just about an important guy in the history of the church and his struggle two thousand years ago, think again! His significance is as strategic as your own eternal destiny. If Peter hadn't been able to get this issue straightened out, it is possible that you and I would not be holding this book in our hands...with hell canceled and heaven guaranteed. Peter's diversion off mission and back to his previous occupation threatened the intended spread of the gospel to all the known world.

It is safe to say that someone else's well-being—and perhaps their eternal destiny—lies in the balances of your response to Christ's final question to Peter.

Chapter Three

MOMENT
OF DECISION

...rescue the perishing

Gary sprawled facedown on the ground, pleading with the armed guard to let him into the room. All he could see beyond the doorway, beyond the firmly planted boots of the guard, were his wife's motionless feet. And the blood.

In that moment, with his face in the dirt, shaking under the crushing blow of this horror, he knew that he must decide. Would he, could he, forgive the terrorist who had shot Bonnie three times in the face? Or would he vow revenge for her blood—even if it took him the rest of his life?

Gary and Bonnie met as college students at Moody Bible Institute. Following graduation and marriage, they committed their lives to take the good news of Jesus to people in one of the more dangerous spots in the world,

Sidon, Lebanon. Although they knew it was not a safe place, Gary had never expected—could never have anticipated—*this*.

Bonnie had left early in the morning of November 21, 2002, to open the clinic where she cared for and ministered to the children of refugees. Hearing a knock at the door, she opened it to the flashing image of a pistol that fired its lethal shots at point-blank range into her face, immediately extinguishing her life. She dropped to the floor, a young, modern-day martyr.

Moments later the phone rang in Gary's bedroom, waking him after a late night of ministry. The panicked voice on the other end of the line was almost unintelligible. The only thing he could understand was that something terrible had happened, and that he needed to get to the clinic as quickly as possible. Searching frantically for enough change to pay for a cab, he left their apartment and arrived at the clinic where his worst fears were confirmed. He raced to the front door only to be restrained from entry by the police—and fell to the ground sobbing and begging to see her.

It was then that something extraordinary happened. Even while the confusion of a thousand thoughts swirled in his head, Gary experienced a moment of spiritual clarity. It was as though the black, churning clouds suddenly parted— just for the briefest moment—allowing a shaft of sunlight to pierce the distress and numbing sorrow. Facedown in the dirt, he told the Lord that he would not abandon the call to which he and Bonnie had committed themselves. He would stay the course, and he would forgive the people who had planned and perpetrated this unspeakable act.

It was a high stakes moment. On earth and in heaven. Would Gary stay on mission? God had clearly called him to the needs of the Lebanese people, and he had answered that call…now at great expense.

The feelings that shot through Gary's mind that terrible morning—the compelling seduction of revenge, hate, and despair—threatened the very calling of God on this young man's life. It threatened the ongoing viability of the power of the gospel through him. And that is no small matter.

Whether or not Gary was aware of it, his wife was a casualty of the incessant, unseen struggles between the forces of hell and the kingdom of light. The monstrous murder of his precious wife at the hands of terrorists was simply one of hell's strategies to frustrate and derail the work of God in that troubled corner of the world.

But it wasn't the only strategy.

In fact, the warfare would not end with Bonnie's demise. Phase two in the battle would be to discourage and distract Gary with self-defeating attitudes of self-pity, revenge, and hate. What a great opportunity to get Gary tangled up in the web of the "blame God" game. Gary's failure at this moment…though understandable…would complete the victory for Satan and his legions. The underworld, well aware that their best moments are turned against them by undaunted followers of Jesus, wanted Gary's heart as well as Bonnie's life.

But they lost.

Gary stood his ground.

They couldn't have his heart. He would not let that happen. So he did for the murderers what Jesus had done for him. He forgave them. What they needed most was not Gary's wrath, but his forgiveness—and even more important, the eternal cleansing of the Great Forgiving One. Gary vowed to offer himself afresh to God—with whatever strength he had left in his life. He committed himself to bringing the healing and redemption of Christ to people in need. Regardless. Wherever.

To this day, Gary's resolve remains as fresh as it was in that excruciating moment when his world caved in. As a result, Bonnie's death has been used to motivate thousands of young college students to understand the gravity of their calling as they move into their worlds as redemptive healers. These students are learning, as Bonnie knew so well, that above everything else, no matter where they find themselves, it is people who matter.

What kind of people? People who need to be shepherded toward Jesus. People who need rescue, direction, and hope in the crossfire of a raging battle between heaven and hell. People whom Satan would gladly destroy in his frantic efforts to defame God, and hijack His eternal purpose.

There is one pivotal reality generally lost on most American Christians, living as we do in the comfort of our affluent society. And we are prone to take the call of Jesus into the needs of others far too lightly. The truth that we have lost is that *we are at war!* Not in Iraq or some far-flung terrorist camp. But a right-here-in-our-own-heart war. A war fought against unseen forces literally hell-bent against us—and everyone around us, for that matter. None of us is exempt. The battle rages!

In his book, *Waking the Dead,* John Eldredge writes:

> There is something set against us…. How I've missed this for so long is a mystery to me. Maybe I've overlooked it; maybe I've chosen not to see. We are at war…. This is not Eden…. The world in which we live is a combat zone, a violent clash of kingdoms, a bitter struggle unto the death…. You were born into a world at war and you will live all your days in the midst of a great battle,

involving all the forces of heaven and hell and played out here on earth.[1]

Of course, that's what the apostle Paul wanted us to know when he called us to…

Be strong in the Lord and in the strength of His might. Put on the full armor of God, so that you will be able to stand firm against the schemes of the devil. For our struggle is not against flesh and blood, but against the rulers, against the powers, against the world forces of this darkness, against the spiritual forces of wickedness in the heavenly places. Therefore, take up the full armor of God, so that you will be able to resist in the evil day, and having done everything, to stand firm. (Ephesians 6:10–13)

When we wake up to the reality of this war—like frightened people who have just heard an air-raid siren—we are most prone to dive into our spiritual bomb shelters. Scrambling to find a book, a scheme, or a strategy to help us survive personally, we focus all of our efforts toward making it to the Promised Land unscathed. As important as that may be, it lacks an understanding of the extent of our calling in the midst of this cosmic struggle.

What about the others around us?

Is this really an every-man-for-himself affair?

Casualties are in the making all around us. From our spouses to our friends, our children, our spiritual leaders, those we work with and come into casual relationships with. The issue is…do we care? Will any of us make an effort to lend a helping hand; to support, shield, or rescue?

In fact, Paul ended his treatise on the war and its armor by asking the Ephesians to…"be on the alert with all perseverance and petition for all the saints, and pray on my behalf" (6:18–19). In Galatians he writes, "If a man is overtaken in any trespass, you who are spiritual restore such a one in a spirit of gentleness…. Bear one another's burdens" (Galatians 6:1–2, NKJV).

This battle is not just about me. It is not about you. It's about us!

Throughout the history of warfare, medals of honor have been awarded to those who have distinguished themselves by risking their own lives to rescue a wounded comrade through heavy fire. These medals come in many shapes and sizes, but ours is in the shape of a bloodstained cross. For it was our leader Jesus who made a way for us to escape to safety as He threw Himself into harm's way to rescue unworthy sinners like you and me from the death grip of Beelzebub, prince of darkness.

And it's not always risking something big in a high-stakes people crisis. Sometimes—in fact, more often—it's about passing a piece of bread to a fellow soldier in need as you sit in the trenches of everyday life. An encouraging word. A note in the mail. Holding friends accountable. Giving the gift of forgiveness. Patience and long-suffering with their faults and struggles. An assurance of regular prayer on their behalf. Babysitting.

Throughout my ministry life many have said to me, "I pray for you regularly." Some, recognizing that spiritual leaders are often special targets in the warfare, tell me they hold me up in prayer every single day. Sometimes as I fall into bed at night, I wonder how I got through the day with all of its challenges unscathed. Sometimes I reflect on a temptation of word, thought, or deed that I refused to give in to. When I wonder how I made it through, I remember my fellow soldiers who stayed on calling, and at some time that day pled for my safety and survival.

Ministry is a fast-paced, busy, multitasked affair. So is your life, I am sure. But the demands of serving God and His people can distract us from our priorities, and threaten some of our most valued and important relationships in our lives. Back in the busiest days of our pastoring, I remember people in our church who would babysit our children—so that Martie and I could get away for a couple of days to regroup and deepen our love for each other. These willing child care experts invested in guarding our hearts against the possibility of a faltering marriage.

In those early days when all our money was obligated before we got it, dinner out meant some generic fast-food experience. Except when Bill and Dorothy Eidson would call us and take us out for a posh steak dinner! The encouragement helped to prepare us to serve another day.

Let's face it, when life is about over, it won't be how successful or satisfied you have been with yourself that will provide the most rewarding memories and experiences. It will be what you have done for others that will fill your heart with a sense of worth and value.

At the end of the day (or the end of life), it is people who will be the source of your greatest reward...or your deepest regret. And what you do with this book—more important, what you do with the call of Jesus on your life—will determine how great that reward...or how profound that regret.

This book is about being in the business of people and staying with it.

For Jesus' sake.

Few of us will ever come close to facing the deep issues that Gary faced in that terrible moment of decisive victory. But if you are reading this book as a follower of Jesus, the dynamics of that moment flash across the screen of your life

on a daily basis. The call of Christ on all of our lives is to
intervene for His sake in the lives of people. People who are
vulnerable in the conflict or being taken down in the warfare. Each day we live we are offered an opportunity to play
a part in that struggle.

The choice to make a difference is always there, waiting
to be seized. The choice to respond with grace and patience
to grumpy, critical, offensive, or threatening people in our
lives. The choice to refuse viewing others as pawns in the
pursuit of our dreams and desires, or as objects of our own
pleasure. The choice to forgive cruel or even unintended
offenses. The choice to master the art of loving our enemies
and extending grace to the undeserving. The choice to be
high on compassion and low on consternation. High on
mercy and low on mad. High on generosity and low on
greed.

We cannot miss the fact that when Jesus called Peter,
Andrew, and the other fishermen, James and John, He
made it clear that He intended to reengineer their calling in
life. From that day forward, their priority would transfer
from the enterprise of catching fish to serving people—
their needs and their eternal destinies.

Jesus understood the awesome dimensions and impli-
cations of that shift in focus. He knew how desperately
people needed what He had to offer: rescue, healing,
redemption, reconciliation, peace, and life. He also knew—

in a way that His disciples could never know—that without intervention these same people would live out their lives as helpless pawns of the destroyer.

1. John Eldredge, *Waking the Dead* (Nashville, TN: Thomas Nelson Publishers, 2003), 13.

Chapter Four

EMBRACING THE CALL (AGAIN)

…three steps from fish to Jesus

Let's be fair with Peter.

This drift off calling was clearly about more than his crushing discouragement with people and his feelings of failure. His "back to fishing" choice was also about some very pressing needs in his life.

Inevitably, in the people business, you will hear your heart cry, "Hey, what about me?" At that point, if you're not careful, you may find yourself scrambling to meet your own needs at the expense of others. You will forget that Jesus has promised to care for your needs as you serve Him.

Peter went back to his career of fishing for all the reasons we have been learning…but among them was the reality that he and the disciples were broke!

Judas had absconded with the treasury. What were the disciples supposed to do? Where would they get money to carry on the ministry? And Jesus? Well, no one had seen much of Him lately. It was becoming increasingly clear that there wasn't going to be any more feeding of the five thousand—let alone the leftover eleven.

Nothing seemed very certain or very clear in those strange, strained days. Ah, but fish….the fish were still there in the sea, waiting to be caught and cashed out. Like always.

For Peter, fish were now the necessity. Providing for the next meal and having enough money to buy what they needed for life now became paramount to the disciples.

Watch out for the "necessities" of life. In our pursuit of the good life the list of necessities can become distorted real fast. What we think is necessary may be far less important than the needs of those around us. In fact, what seems necessary to us may actually be a luxury compared to strategic opportunities to bless others. To my regret, I've had to learn some of the truths the hard way.

Every dad wants a basketball hoop at the end of the driveway. It's a requirement of parental passage to prove you are committed to providing the best for your kids! I am no exception, so my son and I set out one Saturday to find the right kit. The next stop was the hardware store for a bag of cement. Thirty minutes later, I was pounding a posthole digger into the ground, and pouring wet cement around the apparatus that would soon stand proudly in its place: a gleaming monument to father-son togetherness.

But that's not exactly the way it turned out. As someone well said, "The road to hell is paved with good intentions." As laudable as my intentions may have been, I found it difficult to find the time to join Joe Jr. for after-school hoops.

To begin with, there was the lawn....

I have always been obsessed with having a well-trimmed, weedless, green-to-the-death kind of lawn. I am lost in a happy glow whenever I am cutting, trimming, fertilizing, and standing back to admire my artistry. (I know, I'm not well.) Given my need to manicure my lawn to the max, I invested my rare evenings at home in grass world, letting my son's frequent requests for games of one-on-one and H-O-R-S-E go mostly unheeded.

In addition to my landscape obsession, I was pastoring a church at that time. And that meant unscheduled crises and emergencies that soaked up what little discretionary time was left in my schedule. I'll never forget the day I was called to the hospital to sit with one of our families. Their son, about the age of my son, was hanging in the balance between life and death. We waited, prayed, and hoped for the best. But it was not to be. Their son died that afternoon.

As I was driving home from the hospital my values went through a wash of guilt. *What if it had been my boy? What if it had been Joe Jr.?* The pain that gripped my chest in that moment was so real I felt as if it could have been my Joe in that hospital. My Joe on the way to the funeral home.

As I turned down our street, my yard was the envy of the neighborhood. Deep emerald green. Its edges ruler straight. Its smooth expanse free of weeds. Like a golf course. Like a poster for a home and garden show. No one's lawn topped mine. Pulling into my driveway, the first thing I saw was the lonely basketball hoop, casting its long shadow across that picture-perfect grass.

And my heart sank like a stone.

Sitting in my car, staring at the quiet backboard and net, I suddenly hated my lawn. Every after-work hour spent on that pitiful square of turf had robbed me of valuable time I could have spent with my son. I was sick inside that I could have been so shallow to be distracted from what was truly important in life by grass. Grass that as soon as winter arrived would look as lame as the rest of the withered lawns on the street. How much better it would have been to pave it over with concrete and paint it green, rather than neglect never-to-be-redeemed time with my boy.

There was still some daylight left in that warm summer evening, so I rushed into the house and called to him. "Joe? You here? Want to play some one-on-one?" From his room, through the door, I heard the crushing words. "Sorry, Dad, I can't come now. I'm busy."

This may be a good point to throw out a question. *What are the lawns in your life?* Your hobby? Your career? Your easy evenings in the swivel chair? Your social life with that "in crowd"? Your dreams for all that is bigger and better, newer and faster?

I don't know what your lawns are. I just know that we all have them!

And who is it in your life whose needs have been eclipsed by the withering grass of life on your own terms? A friend in need? Your wife? Your husband? Your children? A neighbor in need? A colleague at work? A widow? An orphan?

In Peter's terms, it wasn't the lawn, it was fish.

He had traded his great potential to take the healing, rescuing, encouraging, and liberating gifts of grace to people in his world…for fish. Fish were a way to take care of himself, to meet his own needs. They were easier. More predictable. More what he liked to do. More what he thought was necessary!

But Jesus was not ready to let Peter go.

And He's not ready to let you go, either.

Jesus' first question to Peter has an interesting twist. "Simon, son of John, do you love Me more than these?"

More than who? More than what? At first thought it would seem that Jesus was asking Peter if he loved Him more than Thomas or James or John did. But that is highly unlikely. Jesus had never been pleased by the competitiveness among His disciples—which one of them would be greatest in the kingdom, etc. At that weighty moment, it is doubtful He would want to launch another contest of comparison.

What, then, was Christ saying when He asked about loving Him more than these?

There was only one thing left on the beach.

The fish! One hundred fifty-three scaly, smelly fish!

Did Peter love fish—did he love his old life, his old ways, his old comforts—more than he loved His Lord?

I can't imagine Peter saying at this point, "Actually, Lord, I like You a lot but I really am into fish at this stage of my life!" Of course not. But I do wonder if that is what Jesus hears from our hearts as He challenges us about living out our love for Him into the lives of others.

Did you ever wonder why Jesus selected Peter out of all of them to interrogate in such a penetrating way? Didn't the others count? Didn't Jesus care if they loved Him? Of course He cared. But Peter had been the instigator. It was his idea to set aside the enterprise of the kingdom for nets and bobbers. But as they all sat there on the beach, finishing up their fish sandwiches, totally absorbed in the conversation between Peter and their Lord, you can bet they got the point. It's like spanking your oldest child; the younger ones shape up without a word. Peter was pivotal.

What I find fascinating and particularly helpful is the context into which these questions are spoken. In the story, Jesus challenges Peter's failure on three fronts. Each one is intended to transition Peter from fishing to the enterprise of people. These three dynamics create steps for us as well. Steps back to a love for Jesus that touches His heart and blesses those who cross the path of our existence.

1. Embrace the call again.

Peter and the rest of his crew had fished all night and caught nothing. (I can hardly resist noting that when we launch out on life on our own terms, it inevitably amounts to a disappointing catch!) I wonder if, as dawn broke across the still sea and mist rolled off the hills, those discouraged disciples flashed back to other scenes so fresh in their minds. On those very hills surrounding the lake, Jesus had healed the sick, fed the five thousand, and taught with spellbinding authority. The memories of days gone by must have weighed heavy on their hearts.

But over on the shore, a moving figure caught their eye. A man. Another fisherman, perhaps? A lonely beachcomber, taking a morning walk? They had no idea that it was their resurrected Lord.

The stranger on the shore shouted to them over the water. What was he saying? Ah yes, the typical "Any luck?" sort of question. Perhaps slightly irritated at the query (and embarrassed to admit that they'd had no luck at all), they shouted back a simple "No!"

The stranger then suggested they throw the net on the other side of the boat, and…you know the rest of the story. John (and it wasn't rocket science) said to Peter, "It's the Lord!"

At that point the text says that Peter put on his robes and jumped overboard (again), sloshing through the shallows to meet Jesus on the shore.

Why was it Peter who went overboard? Why the rush to Jesus while the others rowed the boat ashore, dragging the nets overflowing with flopping fish?

Because the Man on shore had just repeated a signature miracle with haunting significance for Peter. How could he forget that day when three years earlier, the Teacher stepped into his boat and asked him to row out a little way from shore while He taught the crowds? When the teaching was over, the Rabbi asked him how fishing had been. Peter admitted that business was not too good. They had "fished all night and caught nothing." In response, Jesus said, "Put out into the deep water and let down your nets for a catch" (Luke 5:4). Luke goes on to tell us that...

> When they had done this, they enclosed a great quantity of fish, and their nets began to break; so they signaled to their partners in the other boat for them to come and help them. And they came and filled both of the boats, so that they began to sink. (vv. 6–7)

Stunned and afraid, Peter fell on his face in the bottom of the boat at Jesus' feet, pleading, "Go away from me Lord, for I am a sinful man!" (v. 8). It was then that he heard those words that would define his calling—and the rest of his life: "Do not fear, from now on you will be catching men" (v. 10).

And now, in the very moment of Peter's backward slide

into his pre-calling life, Jesus showed up on the beach with the identical miracle. Struck by the memory of his life-changing encounter with Christ three years earlier, Peter hurried back to Jesus to rekindle the call afresh.

Can you remember when you first came to Jesus, and felt the healing, cleansing touch of His liberating grace? When you told Him you would follow Him and embrace His cause and live to serve His mission? It might be good to ask yourself, what has changed? Has Jesus changed? Is His mission of no present value? Have the needs of people around your life changed?

Or have you changed?

What would it take for you in this moment to bow your head and embrace the call as though it were as new today? Jesus will meet you, right here in the pages of this book. If you let Him, He will rekindle a love for Him in your inner being that is so deep and true you will gladly join Him once more in the business He takes more seriously than anything else: rescuing, redeeming, and nurturing people.

Step one in answer to Jesus' final question is to *embrace the call again!*

2. Bring your failures to Him.

In a real sense, Peter was not the same man who had first encountered the power and authority of Christ in his fishing boat five feet from shore. Since that time, he had failed repeatedly. And just days before the climactic encounter on the beach, he had done the very thing he had sworn he would never do. Would rather die than do.

He had betrayed His Lord, denying Him in the face of ridiculing enemies. How astounding that Jesus would even want to show up and still be interested in Peter's love and partnership! But there He was. Standing on the shore. Waiting. Wanting Peter back.

In the Bible, even the smallest details can be significant. Such is the case with the notation in John 21:9 that Jesus had built a charcoal fire on the beach. It seems strange that John would have included such an insignificant detail. Why not just say that Jesus had built a fire? Who cares what fueled it?

Peter would have cared. For very good reason.

The word *charcoal* is used only twice in all the New Testament. One instance is here, along the shore of the Sea of Tiberias. And the only other instance (do you remember?) was in Caiaphas's courtyard…at the fire where Peter warmed himself as he disavowed any relationship to his suffering Friend.

Charcoal… Aromas have a way of bringing back memories, don't they? Burning leaves in the fall recall dozens of childhood memories for me. The smell of fresh cut grass reminds me of golf. Catching a whiff of your mother's favorite perfume as someone walks by triggers all kinds of thoughts about home and growing up.

I can't help but think that the pungent smell of that charcoal fire flooded Peter's heart with thoughts about his recent failure. By any other reasonable standard, that act of cowardice should have disqualified him for any future association with Christ or His people.

That's what you would think.

But that's not what Jesus thought.

In the eyes of Christ, Peter's collapse did not disqualify him from being forgiven and useable again for kingdom service. I can't help but believe that Jesus not only needed Peter to get back on calling, but that He missed His impulsive friend, and took the initiative to welcome him back. Even in the face of miserable failure.

Jesus knows. He knows your failures, your disabling weaknesses, your secret idolatries. He is fully aware of how you have blown it with people in the past. Nothing, not one detail, escapes His notice. Even so, He wants to cleanse and use you. He longs for your love again. Come just as you are and let Him lead you in the paths of righteousness. Come and go with Him to the needs and nurture of people.

After all, if He wasn't interested in failures He would have no followers.

The words of a hymn I grew up singing form a fitting

prayer: "*Stoop to my weakness, mighty as Thou art, and help me love You as I ought to love!*"

Step two in answer to His final question is to *bring your failures to Him*. Regardless of who you are or where you have been, Jesus wants you back to the enterprise of the kingdom, cleansed and ready to make a difference in peoples' lives!

3. Trust Him to provide.

There is one very tender, mostly overlooked detail in this story about the reunion on the beach.

In fact, it is a miracle.

We have already noted that one of the reasons Peter and the small band of other disciples went back into business for themselves was to provide for their own needs and desires. And that makes this often unnoticed miracle in our story very instructive.

When they landed on the beach, Jesus had already laid a charcoal fire and was grilling fish on it. *Where did those fish come from?* The Jesus who had no boat and no net had made a miraculous catch of His own.

Why?

Because Jesus wanted to make a very strategic point—to them, and to all of us who find ourselves distracted from mission by our own needs and wants.

Jesus is the provider! As we serve Him, He will provide

for us spiritually, physically, materially and in every way. And He will do so *generously*. It's obvious that John, who is telling us this story, is a fisherman. He tells us how many fish there are in their nets. One hundred fifty three of them. And note that he also adds they are "large" fish. Far from being a net full of mere "keepers," these were trophies! Our Lord's grace is not only sufficient, He is able to provide exceedingly abundantly above all that we ask or think. And as He had already told His disciples, if they would seek the kingdom, all their needs would be cared for. As He said, "Your Father knows you have need of these things."

You may go off mission for personal gain or to meet your own needs, but it is never a reason. Only an excuse.

Jesus provides!

He provides the grace that will sustain and revitalize you. When you don't know what to do next, He provides wisdom. When you have given yourself away to others, He will care for you with special fellowship with Him or through the love and care of another that He sends your way. When you are out of cash, He will supply the very resources you need. When you are pressed for time because you've given up several hours to help someone, He will make it up to you. It is our calling to serve. It is His joy to supply!

Step three toward an others-oriented life is to *get busy*

in the lives of men and women, and trust God to provide and protect.

Reclaim your calling as a follower! Come for cleansing and restoration from your past failures! Trust Him to supply for your needs as you give to the needs of others! And get busy. He will experience your love as you reach out to love others.

Chapter Five

CARING ABOUT
WHAT HE
CARES ABOUT

...and seeing people in a whole new light

Waves lapped the shoreline, the charcoal glowed on the sand, and the rising sun melted away the night shadows.

A peaceful, tranquil setting, perhaps, but something extremely significant would happen on that lonely Galilee beach over two thousand years ago. Jesus was about to teach Peter an unforgettable lesson. And it was this: When you turn your back on people, you in essence have turned your back on Him.

That is a sobering thought. If you love Jesus you will prove it by actively caring for people. If you don't prioritize the needs and nurture of people in your daily activities, then you have made a clear statement to Jesus, telling how you really feel about Him.

This is a landmark point for those of us who are still saying, "Give me one really good reason to inconvenience my life by reaching out to people!" The really good reason is that you intervene in people's lives not for their sake—or even yours—but for the love of the Lord Jesus.

Let's unwrap Jesus' conversation with Peter. Perhaps we can pick up a clue or two to help us engage with fresh enthusiasm in that wild, wonderful, sometimes bewildering world of people.

Let's go back to John 21, and the drama that unfolded after that early morning fish fry on the beach. At the end of Christ's ministry on earth, He showed up one more time to intercept the disoriented lives of His disciples. His purpose was to direct them back on track for His intended purpose for their lives. His target on this occasion was Peter…but it might as well have been you or me.

> So when they had finished breakfast, Jesus said to Simon Peter, "Simon, son of John, do you love Me more than these?" He said to Him, "Yes, Lord; You know that I love You." He said to him, "Tend My lambs."

He said to him again a second time, "Simon, son of John, do you love Me?" He said to Him, "Yes, Lord; You know that I love You." He said to him, "Shepherd My sheep."

He said to him the third time, "Simon, son of John, do you love Me?" Peter was grieved because He said to him the third time, "Do you love Me?" And he said to Him, "Lord, You know all things; You know that I love You." Jesus said to him, "Tend My sheep." (John 21:15–17)

What was Jesus getting at here? Was He questioning the depth of Peter's love? That's what I'd been taught for years. In fact, I've probably preached sermons from that perspective. A little secret locked in the Greek text is that Peter and Jesus used two different words for love in that exchange. Jesus asked Peter if he *agaped* Him. And Peter answered, "Yes, Lord, I *phileo* You!"

Agape love is the highest kind of love, used most often to describe God's love for us. It is a love that transcends feelings, environment, personal interests, and worthiness to receive it. *Agape* loves willingly—regardless. It is unconditional and absolutely reliable.

Phileo love, on the other hand, is a kind of family love—a brotherly love. It's how you feel about your brother or sister (after you are twenty-five!).

Since Jesus repeats the question, it is easy to assume He is trying to ratchet up Peter's love from the *phileo* level to the higher level of *agape*. Hence, He asks the question a second time. As though Jesus was saying, "Now Peter, listen carefully to what I'm saying…do you *agape* Me?" The problem with this approach is that in the third round of questioning Jesus uses the *phileo* word. Is Jesus then saying, "Well, all right, I'll settle for *phileo* love if that's all you can give Me"? It's just like Jesus to lower the bar of commitment, right? Of course not! I've never known Him to do that.

In fact, the words *agape* and *phileo* are on rare occasion used interchangeably. To Peter's credit, perhaps, he was saying that his love was something more than a love of determined choice. After three intensive years of deep bonding, he truly loved Jesus as a brother. In that culture, the bond of love between siblings was even more important than love for parents.

If the meaning is not in the words, then what's going on here? Why the extended interrogation? Some have speculated that since Peter denied Jesus three times just days earlier, Jesus is reminding Peter of that failure of love and loyalty.

Well, maybe. But in reality the text doesn't tell us why Jesus asked the question three times. What we are sure about, however, is that Jesus didn't accept the mere verbal affirmation of Peter's love. In each case, Jesus drove Peter right past the words *I love you*. It would be the actions of

Peter's life that would prove his love for Christ. And so it is for you and me.

Loving Jesus would mean *caring about what Jesus cared about.* And as we know, He cares first and foremost about people! Their needs and nurture. The welfare of their lives and their eternal destinies.

This may come as a disappointment to some of you, but I lived most of my early years in a non-pet family. The few pet memories that I retain are not all that compelling. I recall begging my parents for a puppy at Christmas, which we then gave away six weeks later because I'd neglected him. Then there was the Easter when someone in my dad's church gave us a bunch of baby chicks. My most vivid memory of that episode was watching my sister accidentally step on one. (I'll spare you the details.)

Come to think of it, my mother did keep a canary for years, but do you know how hard it is to bond with a bird?

So I grew up thinking pets were unnecessary and irrelevant. It was obvious, wasn't it? People who lacked human affection and couldn't make it through life on their own needed to be propped up by a pet. But for the rest of us well-balanced, self-sufficient individuals, pets were not a requirement.

Soon after we got married, however, my new wife suggested getting a dog. Clueless, I let fly with this "only people who can't make it with human relationships need the crutch of a pet" kind of talk. I'm afraid it wasn't my best moment. Nor did it move us to new heights in our fledgling relationship.

I had forgotten that Martie had grown up in a pet family. Her lifelong love was Trudy, a black retriever. Trudy was always there for her. If all her friends had rejected her at school, Trudy was there to welcome her home with tail-wagging affection. When Martie would close her bedroom door and have a good cry, Trudy would be there to lick the tears from her cheeks.

At that uncomfortable moment in our relationship, I had to come to grips with a very important principle: *You express your love to someone by caring about what they care about.*

So guess what?

We bought an Old English sheepdog, and named her Paddington!

As it turned out, it wasn't the initial investment but the upkeep that would prove the depth of my love. Like it or not, this non-dog person would have to love the dog to communicate love for Martie.

So I fed her. Walked her late at night. Cleaned up after her. And wouldn't you know it? She began to steal a piece of my heart.

Paddington's arrival, however, and my subsequent commitment to help Martie maintain and care for her had little to do with the dog.

To me, it was all about Martie.

It was my love for her that engaged me in Dog World. And to this day—though Paddington has gone on to the Big Bone in the Sky—I have never regretted it.

In fact, as a result of learning this "caring about what she cares about" dynamic, my life has been plunged into any number of activities that quite frankly haven't been all that much fun. I've hung miles of wallpaper, painted countless rooms, changed diapers, dusted, and vacuumed. Loving Martie means what it means in any other love relationship—climbing into her world and caring about what she cares about.

That's exactly the point that Jesus is driving home in this text. *If you love Me, you will care about what I care about.*

You've got to love the fact that Jesus uses "sheep" as a word picture for people.

If you know much about sheep at all, the imagery is highly instructive. And not particularly flattering. Sheep are neither strong, fast, or mentally swift. They are extremely vulnerable to predators. They are wanderers and easily lose their way. In fact, they can't even find their way home to the barn on their own without a shepherd to guide them. (Which makes the advice that someone gave to Little Bo Peep really lame! You know… "Leave them alone, and they will come home, wagging their tails behind them." In her dreams, maybe!) Sheep tend to overdrink in fast moving waters, and since their nostrils and mouth are so close, can actually drown themselves in satisfying their thirst.

Quite simply, these are among the more mentally and directionally challenged members of the animal kingdom. They really need help.

Just like people.

People are vulnerable. And headstrong. And foolish. And weak. Apart from the protection of Christ, we are all easy marks for the defeating and debilitating attacks of the spiritual underworld. No matter how well educated, wealthy, or crafty one might be, even the best of us are out of our league when it comes to the forces of the evil one. We are like sheep in need of shepherding!

The point that Jesus was making is that people need help.

And that is what shepherds do.

They help.

They protect, sustain, and rescue sheep who have blundered into thorny thickets while nosing after greener grass.

They pursue little lambs (and old ewes and rams who ought to know better) who have been caught in the pits and snares of life.

Do I hear you thinking that this would be a really good thing for your *pastor* to read? After all, aren't they the shepherds of God's flock?

Well, yes. But it is not only them. Jesus calls all of His followers to shepherd and tend others. And if you think there may not be much glamour to it, you are exactly right. Shepherds of Jesus' day were at the low end of the social stratum. It was often a lonely, unheralded task. But sheep were the source of wealth. As weak and witless as they may have been, they were the backbone of their owner's financial portfolio. In that day, you measured your success and fortune by how many sheep you had, and what condition they were in. Seen from that perspective, shepherds were the stewards of the most valuable commodity in the land.

Get the point?

God's earthside wealth is measured in the valuable commodity of people. They are the only part of His creation that He created in His image. Why? So that He could be glorified through them and find fellowship and satisfaction in them. He has no more important possession. But His treasure is at risk, and we are the shepherds who care for His portfolio. When we do it well, He feels our love.

So here is the liberating truth: Getting involved with people in constructive ways isn't about them at all. It doesn't make any difference if you like them or not; if they deserve your attention or not; if your attention to them is rewarded or not; or even if they misunderstand and respond to your care in negative ways. It isn't really an issue if your wife rides in through the window on a broom, or if your husband's limp body is a fixture on the sofa with a remote surgically embedded in his hand. All of that is totally irrelevant, and can no longer count as a legitimate excuse for checking out of the people business.

You aren't doing it for *them*. You are doing it for Jesus, who *does* deserve all the love you can muster.

Now, I wouldn't recommend that you tell people that your intervention in their lives has nothing to do with them. But in the end, it is Jesus and your heart's desire to please and honor Him that drives you into the arena with people. All kinds of people!

In my years of serving Christ as a pastor and now at Moody Bible Institute, I've had many different kinds of people cross my path. There wasn't one who didn't have some measure of need. In fact, it was quite evident that some were more needy than others. As a friend of mine is fond of saying, "The light always attracts a few bugs!" And quite frankly (if I might admit it to you as a kind of private confession), some of them caused great frustration—and often preoccupied my heart and mind with their criticisms and demands.

I'll never forget the new enthusiasm that lifted my spirits the day I realized that all of these people around my life—both the rewarding ones and the unrewarding—were precious to Jesus! And, *if they are precious to Jesus then they must be precious to me!* They are in fact His prized possessions. He died for each of them. He loves them and desires to lead them to the best…warts and all. And He is looking to me to love Him enough to help get the job done.

How nice it would be if you could "just love Jesus" without the messy, frustrating people-component. I've often thought my Christianity would be a cakewalk if it weren't for people!

Chapter Six

THE PRIORITY
OF PEOPLE

...no one said it would be easy

Clutching his ever present blanket, and with unusual determination in his voice, Linus announced to Lucy he had finally discovered his calling in life. He was going to be a doctor.

Lucy, ever the intimidating big sister, countered that there was no way he could be a doctor because, as she said, he hated mankind.

Stung by that objection, Linus shot back that she really didn't understand. He *loved* mankind. It was people he couldn't stand.

All of us can identify with Linus's dubious distinction. Humankind is a wondrous thing. It's those pesky people who spoil the broth. While often the source of our greatest joys, people are just as likely to use us, frustrate us, cheat us, intimidate us, misunderstand us, criticize us, manipulate us, abuse us, talk behind our backs, ignore us, and inevitably disappoint us.

Most of us have come to realize that people are complex and unpredictable—especially if they're "not like us." Differences in gender, color, culture, and class complicate our desire to find pleasure in relationships. We find ourselves confused and overly cautious when the person who brings us delight in one moment disappoints us the next!

The only way to survive in this people-dangerous world (so we are told) is to take matters into our own hands and make sure that life is all about us—our own dreams, goals, and desires. And when people threaten the trajectory of those dreams, we should jettison them. As quickly as possible. Use those who can help you and eliminate everyone else seems to be the name of the game.

As Paul Simon used to sing, "Just slip out the back, Jack, and set yourself free."

In short, with the exception of several periodic casual and comfortable encounters, living for others—for their needs and nurture—seems far too hazardous. Some of us have learned the hard way that getting involved with people leaves us vulnerable and at risk. Outside of a few close friends who make us feel good about ourselves, and subordinates at work who do what we tell them to and treat us well (to our face), the world of people is often too spooky for us to wade in much further than the shallow end.

Masking our resistance to closer relationships, we salve our neglect by "focusing on Jesus." Sounds good, doesn't it? After all, He's the one we can trust. In relationship with Him (who needs people?), we feel safe, secure, and satisfied.

But we are also way off the mark. And the Lord of our lives is not pleased. Patiently, firmly, repeatedly, He keeps reminding us that our relationship with Him is going nowhere unless it is lived out in a bold, constructive involvement in the lives of others. When Peter affirmed his love for Jesus verbally, Jesus said in essence that He would know that Peter was serious about loving Him when Peter got busy with people. Or, as Jesus actually said it, *"Feed My sheep."* He measures His worth in our lives not by what we say, not by what we sing in heartfelt worship, not by how many rules we keep, but rather by how we treat people and respond to their needs.

One of the Sadducees' lawyers once sought to trap Jesus with a leading question. "Teacher," he asked, "which is the greatest commandment in the law?"

For His answer, Jesus reached all the way back to the first of the Ten Commandments: That we love the Lord our God will our heart, soul, and mind.

We all like that command. It has a nice ring to it. But

then He upped the ante.

The second, He said, was like the first: You should love your neighbor as you love yourself. In other words, *If you say you love God, then the proof of that love rises and falls on what you do with and for your neighbor.*

You're probably saying, "Right, but obviously Jesus doesn't know my neighbor!"

Instead of assuming that the omniscience of Jesus stops at your property line, it would be better if you asked, "Who is my neighbor?"

Brace yourself.

The biblical definition of neighbor, as Jesus uses it in this text, is *anyone who crosses the path of your life*—not just the guy or gal who occupies the space next door. It's that rude person in the "12 Items or Less" line at the grocery store, who makes you late because he has just placed 17 items on the belt. (And you know there are 17 items because you counted them one by one!)

It's your wife. Your husband. Your roommate. Your coworker. It's anyone who comes close enough to be loved and helped.

In His last teaching session with His disciples, Jesus raised the bar even higher with a new command: that they love one another. Surely at a bare minimum, that means we need to get positively involved in the lives of fellow followers. And let's face it, this may be the toughest test yet. Do you ever feel that many people you know who are outside the faith are nicer and easier to love than some of the Christians you know? I'm reminded of the ditty that goes, "To live above with saints we love, oh that will be glory. To live below with saints we know…well, that's a different story!"

But the real issue comes to the surface when Jesus adds this reminder: Others outside of the family will only recognize our link to Him if we live to love each other. That's a good reminder for those of us who for too long have thought that outsiders will know we are Christians because "we don't drink, dance, smoke, chew, or go with girls who do."

After teaching some of these concepts in this book a few months ago, I was approached by a lady after the session. She told me that she and her husband had recently begun attending a small church. Their new fellowship, she noted, put a heavy emphasis on conformity to a list of "lifestyle" rules as long as your arm. Yet at the same time, she added, she had never been in a church where there was more gossip and backstabbing going on.

You can take it to the bank that Jesus is not loved in that place—regardless of what they say or sing, regardless of what Bible translation they preach from the pulpit, regardless of whether their list of rules reaches around the block and back.

Ask yourself this simple question: "What is the primary concern of my life?" For some, the honest answer is personal survival. For others, answers like saving for retirement, making more money, getting ahead at work, snagging that "ideal" date, spending a quiet evening by the fire with a good book, or improving a golf handicap may head the list. The reality is that unconditionally intervening in others' lives to help and heal probably doesn't rank near the top of most of our lists.

And, I would like to add, there is probably nothing wrong with the things on your list. I really do hope to improve my golf handicap! It's just that there is something wrong with any list that does not feature the priority of people at the top.

If you are still wondering if this is really all that important, think of what James says. *The Message* paraphrase puts it like this: "Anyone who sets himself up as 'religious' by talking a good game is self-deceived. This kind of religion is hot air and only hot air. Real religion, the kind that passes muster before God the Father, is this: Reach out to the homeless and loveless in their plight, and guard against corruption from the godless world" (James 1:26-27).

We need to get a grip on the reality that following Jesus

is not always just about "us and Him"; nor is it always a safe and comfortable thing. Yes, it is always a good and ultimately rewarding endeavor to follow Him. But be ready: That path will always lead directly into the lives of others.

At this point I am sure that a lot of objections are surfacing in your heart. Don't be surprised. The adversary wants people for his own destructive purposes without your getting in the way. I know the excuses, because at one time or another, I've been tempted to use them all myself. *He doesn't deserve my care and attention…. Anyway, if I'm nice to her, she'll take advantage of me…. My acts of help will most likely be misunderstood, rejected, criticized, ignored, or unsuccessful…. Besides, what about ME? Who will care for and love me if I start to prioritize the needs of others in my life?… Besides, honestly, I'm usually too tired after I've given it all at the office to do much else besides channel surf in my easy chair.*

No one said it would be easy. In fact, Jesus got involved in the needs of your life and mine all the way to the cross. Which reminds me that when He calls us to follow Him, He also says that we are to take up our cross as well.

Remember! We are not home yet. We are at war, and running rescue operations into the world of people is going to take grit. But as Hebrews tells us, Jesus persevered in the ordeal to rescue our perishing souls for the joy that was set before Him. Think of a brother won, a sister rescued from a fall, the smile on an orphan's face, a friend encouraged, and your six-year-old son hugging your neck and saying, "Dad, I love it when you play ball with me!" The struggle may be periodically challenging, but the rewards are out of this world!

One of my fondest memories as a boy took place late at night after my dad had prayed with me and turned out the lights. I had rescued a discarded old radio and placed it on the nightstand by my bed. After waiting for my dad to get down the hall, I'd turn it on with the volume way down low. By sliding my pillow over to the edge of the bed, I was able to listen with no one else knowing. Into the darkness, a calm and soothing voice would begin his program by singing these words…

> *Somebody cares about you,*
> *And worries till the day comes shining through!*
> *Somebody cares if you sleep well at night,*
> *If your day goes all wrong,*
> *Or if your day goes all right!*
> *Somebody cares about you,*
> *And worries till the sun comes shining through.*
> *Please believe me, it's so,*

But in case you didn't know it,
Somebody cares!

Then he would always say, *"Have no fear, Big Joe is here!"* During the rest of the program, Big Joe took calls from people in need, and arranged ways for their needs to be met.

To my little uncomplicated life, there was a soothing and nourishing feeling in my spirit when I heard Big Joe sing and talk. To me, he seemed like a huge, oversized, soft marshmallow that all the world could fall into and be happy.

Since I grew up just outside of New York City, it strikes me now, as an adult, that in such a large and impersonal city many were lost and alone, overwhelmed by needs in their lives. How healing it must have been to them to hear that somebody cared!

There may even be someone reading this book right now who is holding back the tears, wishing that someone would read these pages and intervene in their lives in a caring way.

Could it be you that they are waiting for?

Chapter Seven

SO MANY PEOPLE, SO LITTLE TIME

…committing intentional acts of love

Here is what we have learned. From Jesus' point of view, only one thing really counts in this world.

People.

God's Son is passionate about rescuing men and women, boys and girls, from the evil designs of the destroyer. He cares about their daily lives and their struggles. He cares about their eternal destiny.

He wept over Jerusalem because He would have gathered them as vulnerable chicks under His wings. He was moved with compassion because, as He saw it, people were distressed and dismayed…like sheep without a shepherd. With His own lips He declared His reason for visiting our broken planet: "For the Son of Man has come to seek and to save that which was lost" (Luke 19:10). Life was never about Him. He didn't have long here, and rescue was always on His mind. If you doubt it, just follow Him.

All the way to the cross.

Outside of stepping aside periodically to rest and pray to re-tank His strength for another run at people, His life was never absorbed with His own interests or making a mark for Himself. In His own words, "The Son of Man did not come to be served, but to serve, and to give His life a ransom for many" (Matthew 20:28).

I don't ever recall Him saying to Judas, His CFO, "Do we have enough money to buy that hill over there? It would make a great place for a Messianic Library after I die, so that people will remember Me and the contribution I have made."

His life was singularly focused on people. He knew better than anyone else that the only commodity at risk in the unseen warfare—and the only entity going all the way into eternity—is people. He was well aware that everything else gets checked at the border.

He lived to prove one profound point: *Only people count.*

And He wants His followers to share His passion and to partner in His mission. When we do, He knows how much we love Him!

So let's connect the dots. First of all let's remind ourselves that we're certainly not lacking in prospects! People are everywhere. The bumper sticker motto of every follower of Jesus ought to be, "So many people, so little time!"

But beware of being too narrow in the target zone of your efforts. Always keep in mind that God's Son reached out to those who were despised, condemned, and hated by seemingly everyone else. He stood beside the woman caught in adultery, as one by one her accusers melted away. He attended parties with hated tax collectors, heavy imbibers, and known prostitutes. He opened His heart and the very doors of heaven to the convicted felon dying on the cross next to His. And not so very long later, He sought out, received, and commissioned Saul of Tarsus, a committed enemy and persecutor of the church.

Jesus took hit after hit for caring about the needs and welfare of those who were considered nonpersons or worse to the religious elite. He didn't write anyone off—unless it was those haughty religious leaders who stubbornly clung to their proud and hypocritical righteousness. Jesus continually stunned His friends and foes alike by the company He kept. When He saw the slightest spark, the slightest inclination toward God-hunger in an individual's soul, nothing else mattered. Not race. Not gender. Not status. Not track record. Not public opinion. Not multiplied failures.

In many respects, caring about people is a calling without boundaries. And the issue is not that you go out of your way and dismantle your priorities to find some rejected soul. It simply means that your heart remains open to whomever it is that God leads across your path. And if that man or woman happens to walk outside the normal stan dards of decency and propriety, you refuse to back away. Instead, you let the love of Jesus flow through your life with intention and resolve.

Are you ready now to engage your world for Jesus? Great. But hold up just for a moment. There are a few simple rules of engagement that you need to keep in mind.

1. You can't help everyone all the time!

It's important to know yourself and to know your limits. Even Jesus left some unhealed and unhelped.

2. Establish your priorities.

For what people are you directly responsible? You can't neglect them for the needs of others. There are concentric circles of care. At the center is your spouse (or, if you are single, it may be a close friend). The next circle represents your children, then your extended family, then your brothers and sisters in Christ, then others who cross your path at work or in the normal course of your daily routine.

3. Step away when you are drained.

You can't minister from an empty tank. Even Jesus went apart to rest awhile. When your tank registers on "Weary," find a way to refresh yourself. And then step back into the people business with new resolve.

4. Be aware of your capacity to help.

Know yourself! Some of us are not equipped to help with in-depth counseling, mental or emotional illness, financial advice, or serious health concerns. There are "holders," "helpers," and "healers" in the body of Christ. Sometimes we can just hold on to people until we can find someone to help them. At others times we can offer limited help until we can get them to someone who can heal them. And sometimes we get the opportunity to do all three.

5. Know that there are some people who will never be helped.

Unfortunately, there are a few people who have learned that the only way to get attention and to feel loved is to have a problem. If that is the case, you can never help them, because their problem is their treasure. If you have spent a lot of time and there are seemingly no improvements or any response to healthy counsel, then you need to graciously bow out and invest your time and talents elsewhere.

In the context of these boundaries, what do you have in your hand? What resources do you bring with which to engage people at their point of need? If you are saying, "Not much," then let me remind you of the boy who brown-bagged it to a revival service. All he had was a little lunch with two fish and five loaves. And, by the way, these were most likely small biscuits of barley and salted dried fish the size of sardines. It wasn't much. But as the old saying goes, "Little is much when God is in it!" Put whatever resource you possess in His hands, and watch it multiply.

Let me suggest some of the resources that every one of us has in our personal bag of need-meeting power.

1. Prayer

I put this first because I'm guessing it might be at the *bottom* of your list—if it made it at all. Periodically someone will ask me, "What can I do to help?" And when I can't come up with anything off the top of my head, they will often say, "Well, I'll just pray." *Just* pray? You must be kidding. Prayer is the power that moves God's heart.

Each summer over three thousand Christians descend on a rather sleepy town in the Lake District of the UK known as Keswick, actually doubling the size of the town. They come for three weeks of worship and study of the

Word at Britain's most historic conference grounds.

Last summer I was asked to participate in the teaching sessions of the first week of the Keswick conference. I started the assignment on Sunday morning by preaching in one of the churches at the outskirts of town. The pastor had asked one of the ladies in the church to come and lead in prayer, and then give her testimony. It all seemed normal enough…until she began to share how she came to know Christ as her Savior.

She told the congregation that she worked in a deli/gift shop in Keswick. Several years previous, during one of the Keswick weeks, a lady attending the conference came into the shop every morning for coffee, and struck up a friendship with her. She admitted that there was something different about this woman, and that at the end of the week she felt sorry that her new friend, Winnie, was leaving to go back to her home. Every year she waited to see Winnie again during the conference weeks, but as the years passed she never came back.

Several years after she had met Winnie, however, she began to have a drawing in her spirit to Jesus that was so strong—so irresistible—that it was almost physical in its power. After trying to dismiss it, she found that it persisted in increasing strength, until one day she wandered into a church. After meeting with the pastor, she accepted the Lord Jesus as her Savior.

A couple of years later, a lady walked into the shop during the conference weeks and asked her if she remembered Winnie from many years before. She lit up at the thought of her long-absent friend, and said that she certainly did remember. She added that long after she had met Winnie, she had come to know Christ as her Lord and Savior! The lady on the other side of the counter gasped in joy, and said she couldn't wait to tell Winnie, *since Winnie had prayed for her salvation every day without fail since she left Keswick years before.*

I could hardly hold back the tears as I listened to this testimony. Every day! Praying and praying for someone you had met years before, until the enemy finally said, "I give up, I can't hold on to her against the power of these persistent prayers." And the way was cleared for Jesus to energize her heart to come to Him.

Then to cap it all off she said, "And I am so glad that Winnie is here this morning," at which point warrior-hero Winnie stood up to the enthusiastic applause of that typically staid English congregation.

As we walked out, I saw her with Winnie walking down the lane and hurried to catch up. Telling them what an encouragement her testimony had been to me, I added that since it took so many years for Winnie's prayer to be answered, Satan must have had a tight grip on this shopkeeper's life. She looked at me with a serious and telling look and said, "I cannot tell you how strong his grip was on my life!"

Winnie is a model of what it means to be undauntedly faithful to the call of rescuing men and women. She persevered in long-distance prayer without a clue of what was going on in the spiritual underworld. The Spirit energized her undaunted commitment to the welfare of others and the battle was won.

Can you in this quiet moment think of a person who rises as a candidate for your first redemptive move?

2. Your spiritual gift

All who have come to Jesus as Savior have been endowed with a special gift to empower and enable you for service. This gift is to be used to bless and help others. There are gifts of *serving, hospitality, mercy, giving, administration, teaching, exhortation, prophecy, etc.* Your gift is your ability to play a constructive role for Christ's sake in the lives of others. But finding and knowing that gift is often a challenge. Someone wisely counseled me years ago that you can know what your gift is by the kind of activity you are naturally drawn to, that you have energy for, that you see fruitfulness in, and that others affirm you in when you exercise it. The way to discover your spiritual gift is to get busy in the people business until you can sense where you are most effective. Don't try to serve apart from your lead gift. It is defeating to try to do things that you are not built to do.

3. Time and attention

We all have the capacity to give both of these commodities away on a regular basis. The most flattering service that a husband and father can give to his wife and kids is his time and attention.

Give a day a month to some enterprise that is effectively helping and reaching people. Ladle soup at the mission. Paint a widow's living room. Change the storm windows for a disabled person. There are lots of opportunities in this category.

4. Money

Most of us do not have the giftedness, calling, or capacity to minister to the homeless, AIDS victims, the disabled, and the orphaned. But that does not mean that we cannot have a part in their need. Pick a ministry that targets and effectively serves and blesses these categories of people. Partner with them in prayer and regular financial support. For years Martie and I have split our giving into two categories. We give our tithe to our local church and then have what we call our 'Special Giving' fund. This extra fund gives us the freedom to save a significant amount of resources to bless and help as needs arise. Try it. It brings us a lot of joy.

5. Grace

Grace is the action of abundant kindness, even to the most undeserving of offenders. Grace forgives, gives space, and doesn't keep score. How is it that we who have been so greatly graced by God are so unwilling to give His grace to others? The most helpful thing you might do today is give someone the love they don't deserve.

6. Encouragement

Sometimes it's real simple and not very demanding. A word of comfort and hope. A call. A card. A passage of Scripture. A hug with no words. A listening ear. An understanding heart.

Can you in the quiet moment think of a person who rises as a candidate for your first redemptive move? There are people all around our lives who need the Lord—and will only find Him through us. There are people who need to be forgiven so that they can have a future, rather than remaining imprisoned to the past. There are people who need to be cared for, in Jesus' name, just as He cares for us. There are people who need to be taken by the hand and led from addictive paths of darkness to the freedom of walking in His light. There are people who need to be strengthened and encouraged. There are people who need to be protected, restored to family and friends, and made to feel whole and valued. Never doubt it: These kinds of people are all around our lives every day.

How close are they? As close as your best Christian friend. As close as your own spouse.

One of the most moving scenes for me in the last movie of the epic *Lord of the Rings* trilogy was when Frodo collapsed on the very slopes of Mount Doom. So near the end of a long, long journey, with their destination at last in view, the ring bearer could go no further. With victory so close at hand in a great battle of good against evil, the forces of evil were about to win. Frodo's faithful companion, Sam, pleaded with his friend to get up and keep going—to finish the task before it was too late. When his fellow hobbit wouldn't or couldn't stir, Sam, himself exhausted beyond words, said, "Mr. Frodo, I can't do it for you, but I can pick you up and take you there."

Struggling, Sam picked Frodo up and carried him to the heart of Mount Doom, where victory would finally be won.

At one time or another, each of us needs a Sam. We need someone to be there to rescue us at the brink of failure, to communicate confidence and worth in the face of impending defeat and discouragement.

When Martie and I saw *The Return of the King*, I was

going through a particularly challenging time, and found myself often plagued with confusing, disheartening thoughts and feelings. Since people have this weird sense that people who do what I do don't wrestle with discouragement, I often feel deeply alone in times like these. When my heart is down, I feel that I have far more critics than champions, and I find my spirit longing for a champion to carry and wave my flag. (I know that Jesus is my champion, but there are times when you need Him to incarnate His love and care in the skin of a fellow believer.) Perhaps that's why I identified so quickly with Sam's loving willingness to carry the battle-weary Frodo.

I so desperately wanted and needed a Sam!

I had been sharing with Martie some of my internal struggle just the day before, and her input had been a great help. As we walked from the theater, I said, "I feel like I need a Sam."

She grabbed my arm and pulled me close. With delight in her eyes and voice, she said, "I'm your Sam!"

I will never forget the depth of meaning that her words and the love in her eyes had on my heart. The person who knew me and loved me more than anyone else had just pledged herself afresh to lift me up and strengthen me for the journey. Just knowing that was a wind of healing to my soul. I was not alone!

Think of what God said to Israel: "The LORD your

God carried you, just as a man carries his son, in all the way which you have walked until you came to this place…. Even to your old age…I will carry you…and I will deliver you" (Deuteronomy 1:31; Isaiah 46:4).

Actually our calling to get involved in redemptive ways in people's lives is nothing more than the high privilege of being to others what God is to us—what He would be to them if He were here in physical presence.

As you read these words on this page, all kinds of people are fighting all kinds of battles with the enemy of their soul. And they are waiting for the supernatural rescue Jesus seeks to offer them through us.

Have you ever wondered why you got stuck with so many weird and troublesome people in and around your life? God may have placed you, as His frontline soldier, on a frontier where a breakthrough of divine love would make all the difference. As you allow Him to rescue and love and shepherd through you, you may find yourself participating in a most dramatic victory against the underworld. You get to be the warrior hero!

Don't flinch at that designation. There is a lot at stake here. And thankfully, you don't do it alone. *All you do is to remain faithful to the call to live for the care and rescue of people.* For His part, the Spirit of God will energize your obedience to victory! Welcome back to the world of people!

BIG CHANGE

SMALL BOOKS
BIG CHANGE

www.bigchangemoments.com

BIG CHANGE

SMALL BOOKS
BIG CHANGE

www.bigchangemoments.com

BIG CHANGE

THE TREASURE PRINCIPLE
Discovering the Secret of Joyful Giving
RANDY ALCORN ISBN 1-57673-780-2

THE TREASURE PRINCIPLE BIBLE STUDY
BRIAN SMITH & RANDY ALCORN
ISBN 1-59052-187-0

SECRETS OF THE VINE
Breaking Through to Abundance
BRUCE WILKINSON 1-57673-975-9

SECRETS OF THE VINE FOR WOMEN
DARLENE MARIE WILKINSON
ISBN 1-59052-156-0

THE PRAYER OF JABEZ
Breaking Through to the Blessed Life
BRUCE WILKINSON ISBN 1-57673-733-0

THE PRAYER OF JABEZ FOR WOMEN
DARLENE MARIE WILKINSON
ISBN 1-57673-962-7

**For a complete list of Big Change titles,
visit our website at www.bigchangemoments.com**